I0488977

Unleashing Creativity With Flower Mandalas Coloring Book

Flower Mandala Coloring Book for Creative Types

Flower Mandala

By : Gala Publication

2

Published By :

Gala Publication
© Copyright 2015 – Gala Publication

ISBN-13: **978-1522722144**
ISBN-10: **1522722149**

Design 1

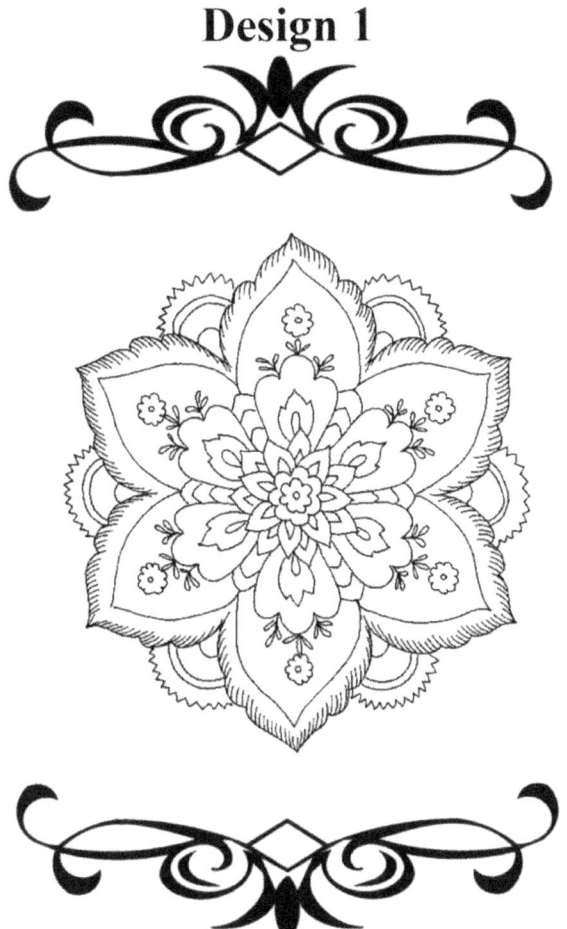

Design 2

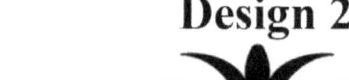

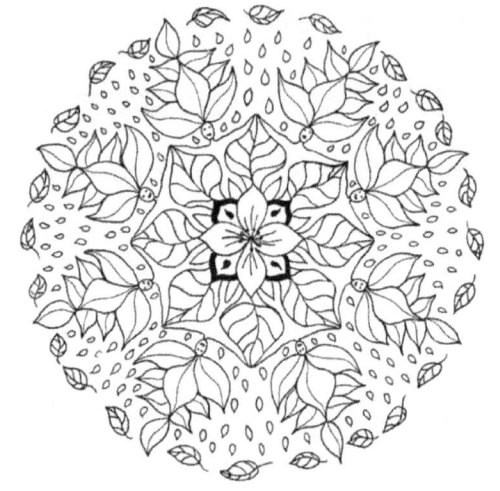

Design 3

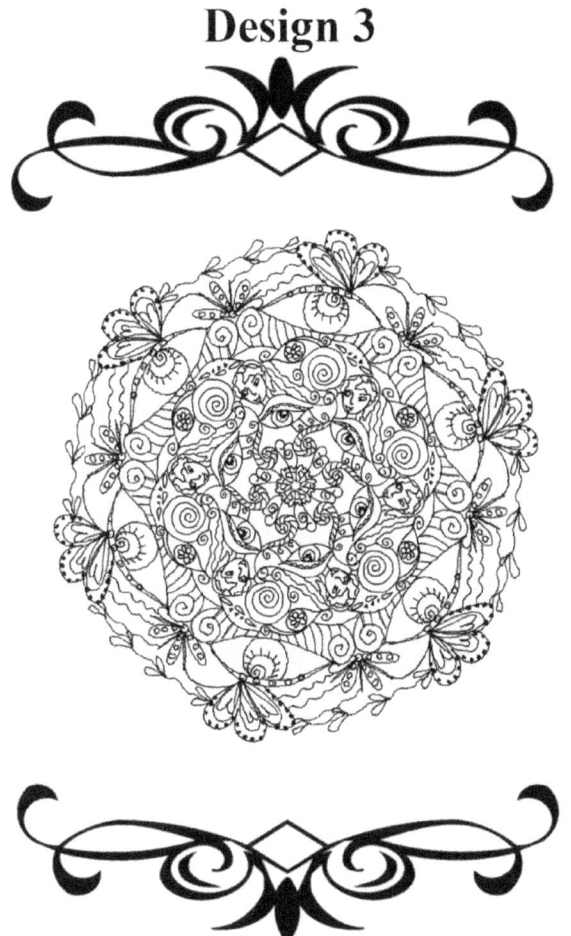

Design 4

Design 5

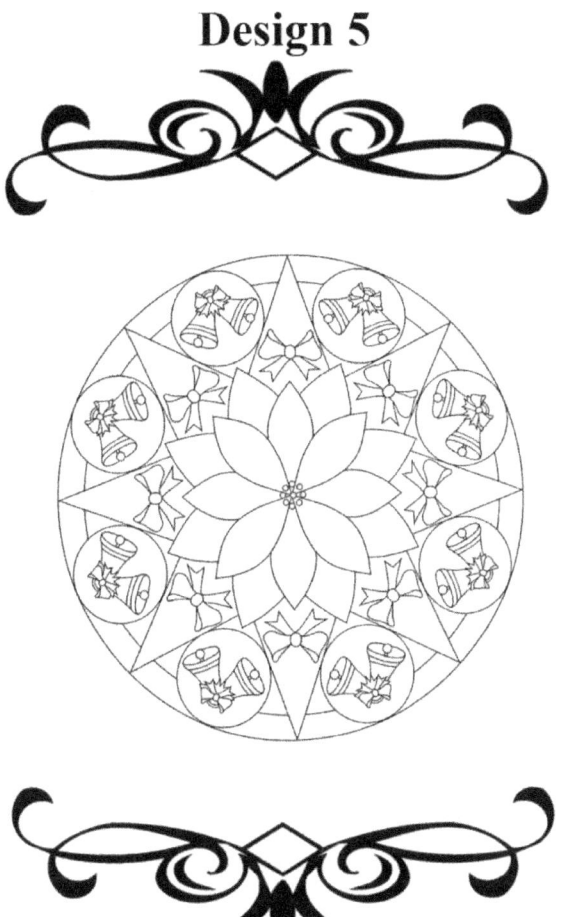

Design 6

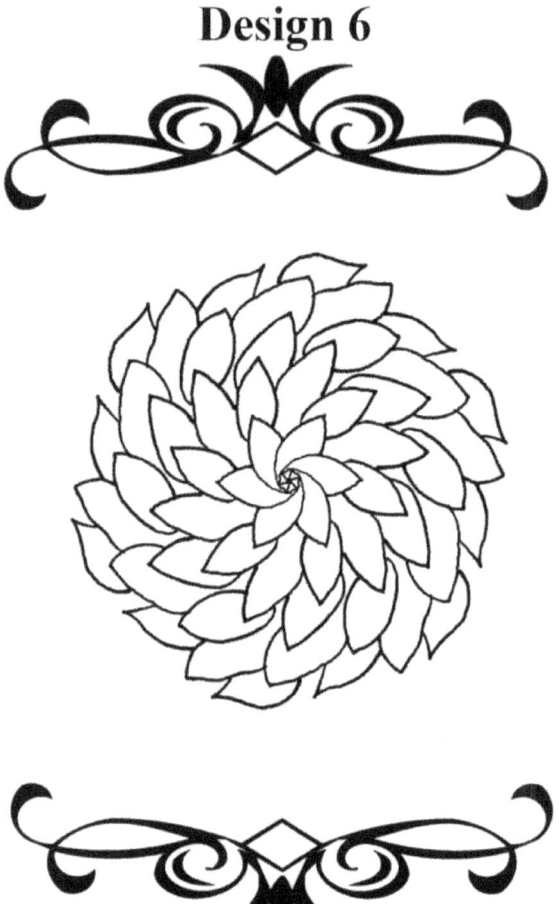

Design 7

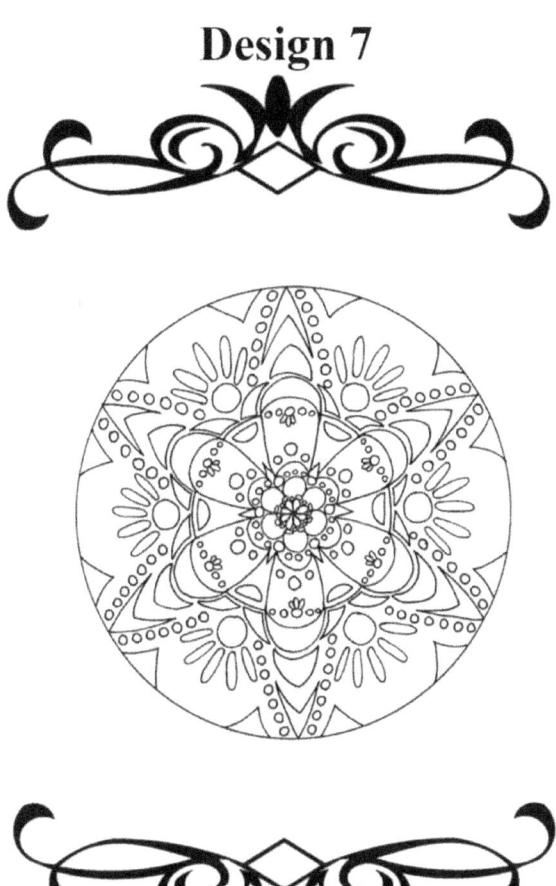

Design 8

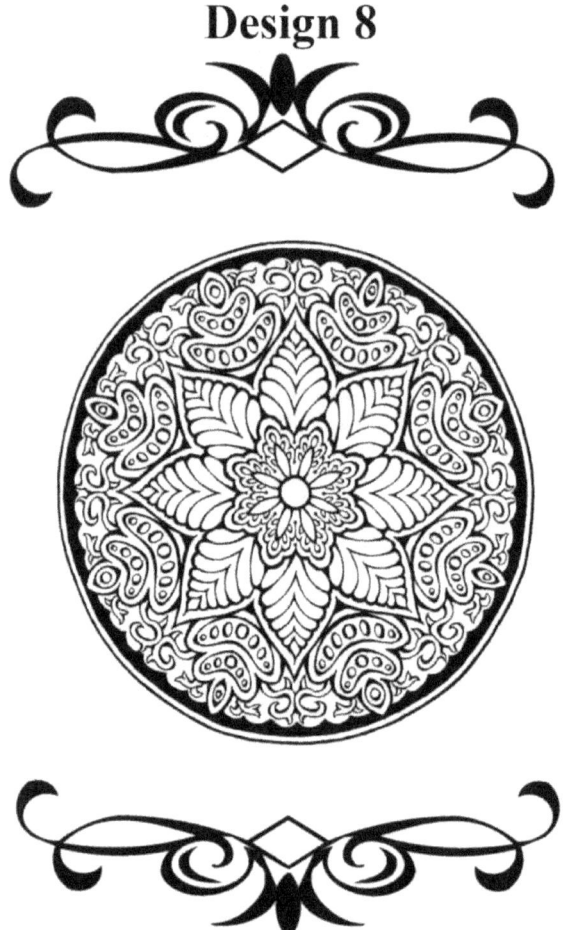

Design 9

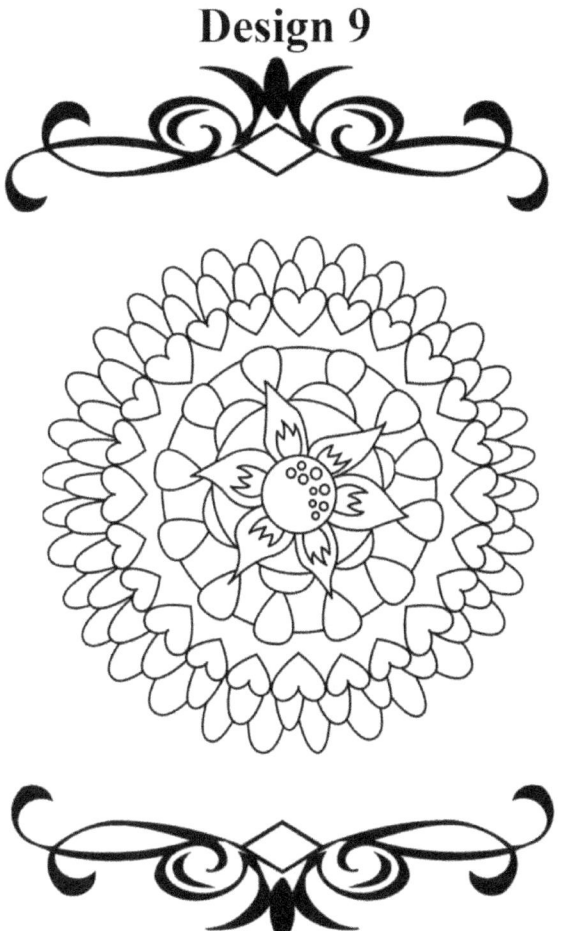

Design 10

Design 11

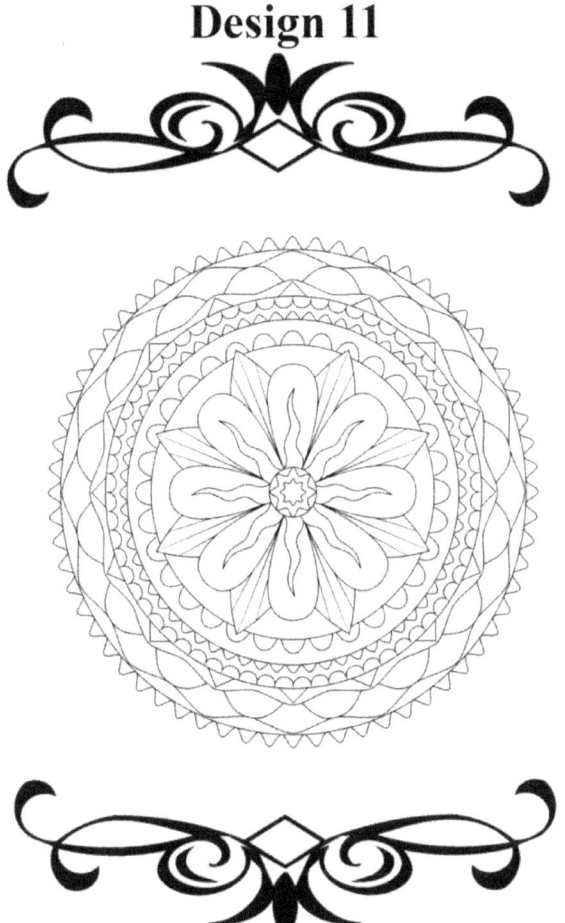

Design 12

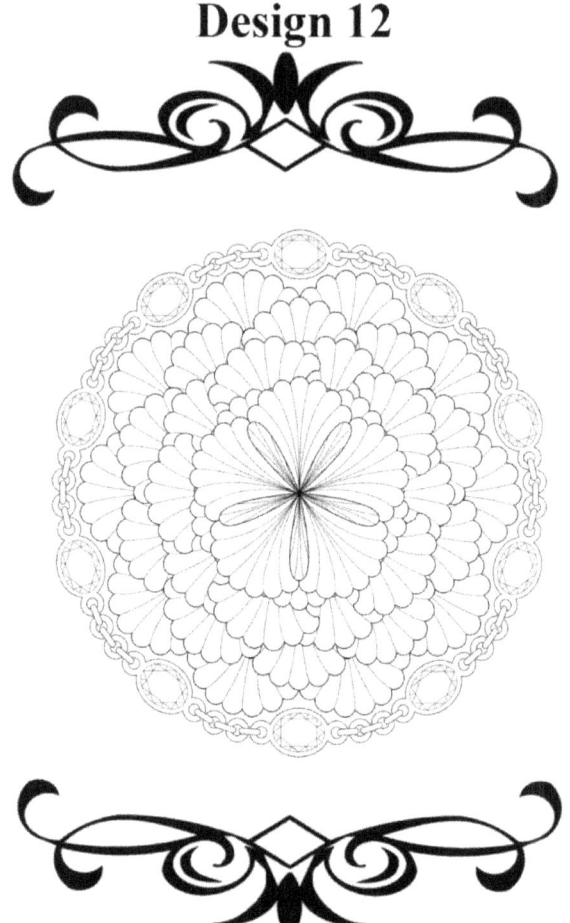

Design 13

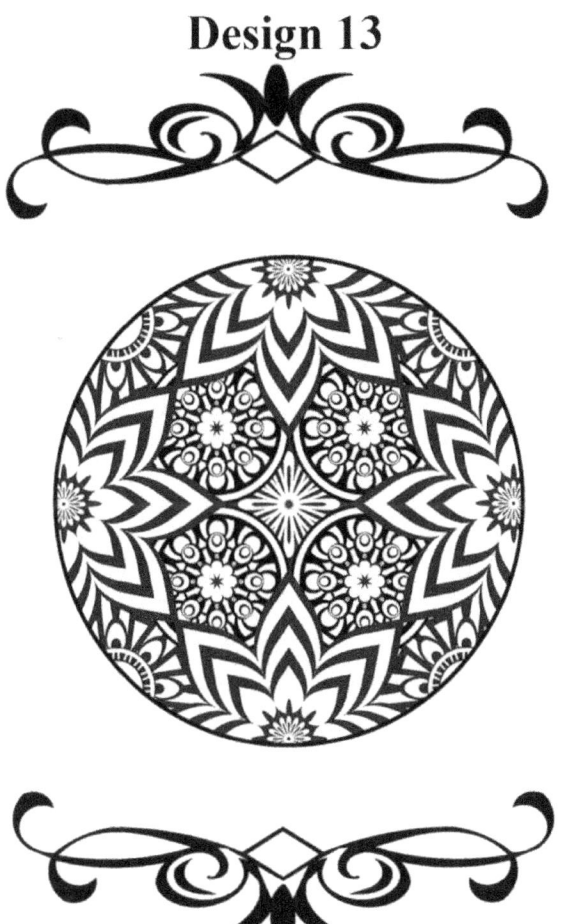

Design 14

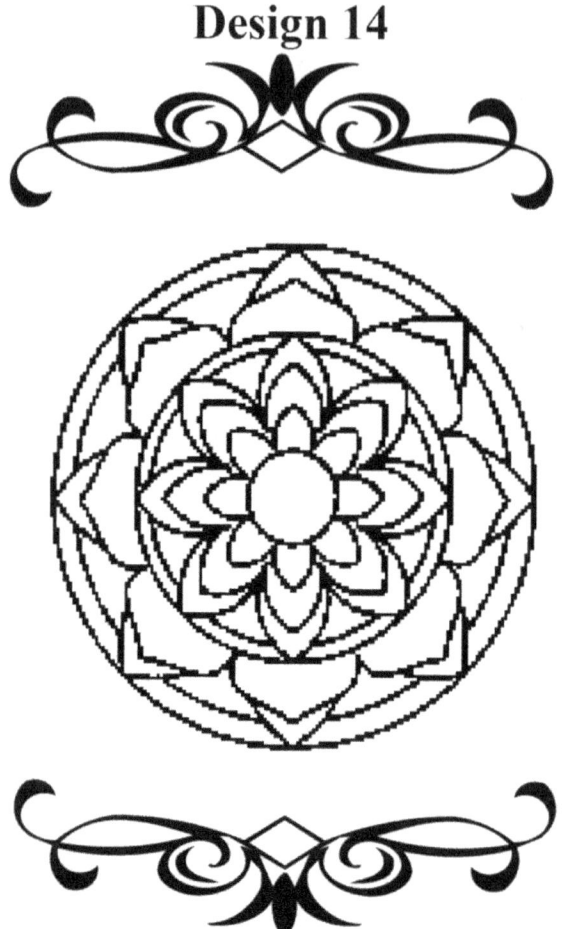

Design 15

Design 16

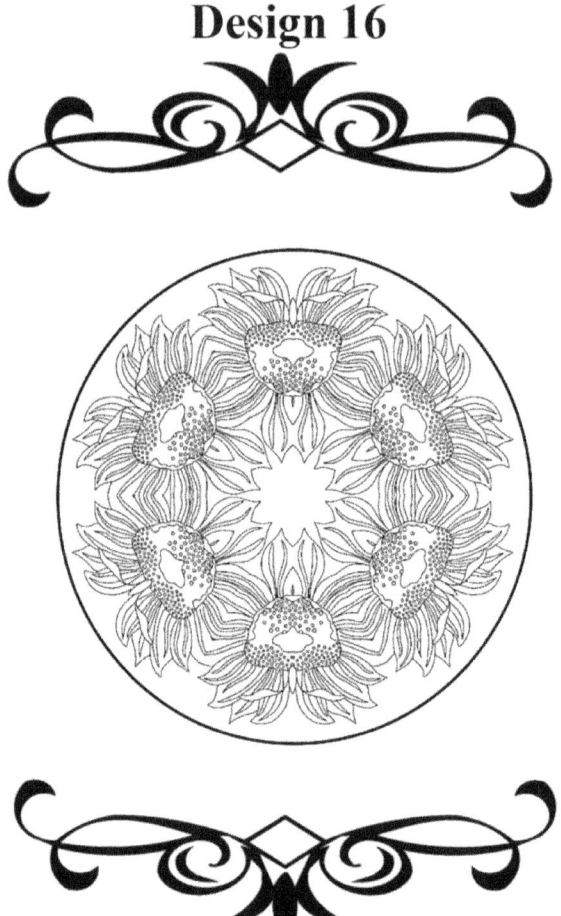

Design 17

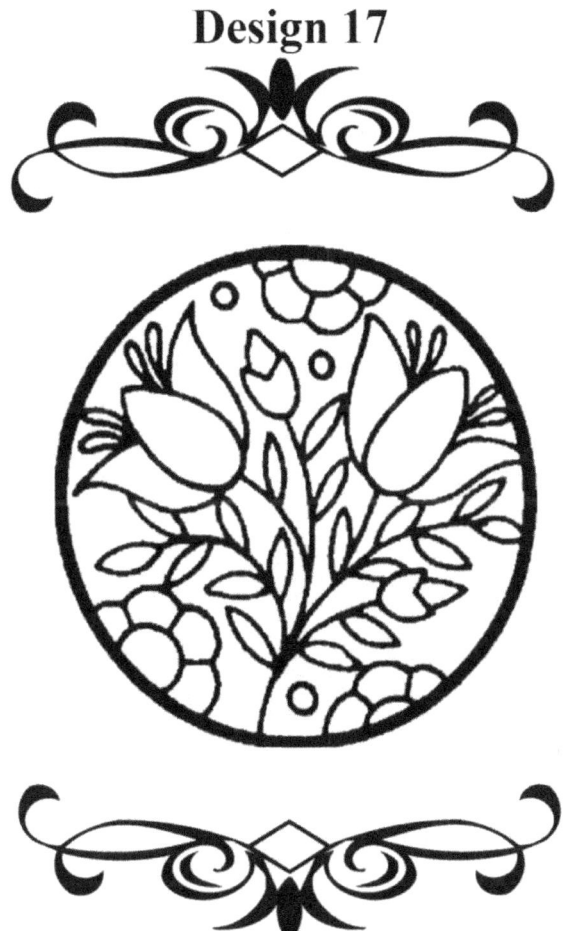

Design 18

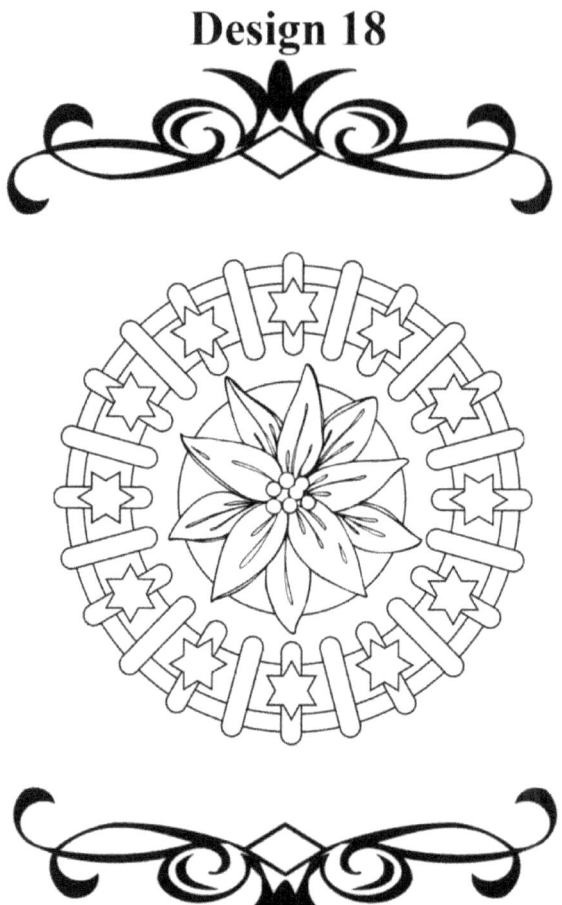

Design 19

Design 20

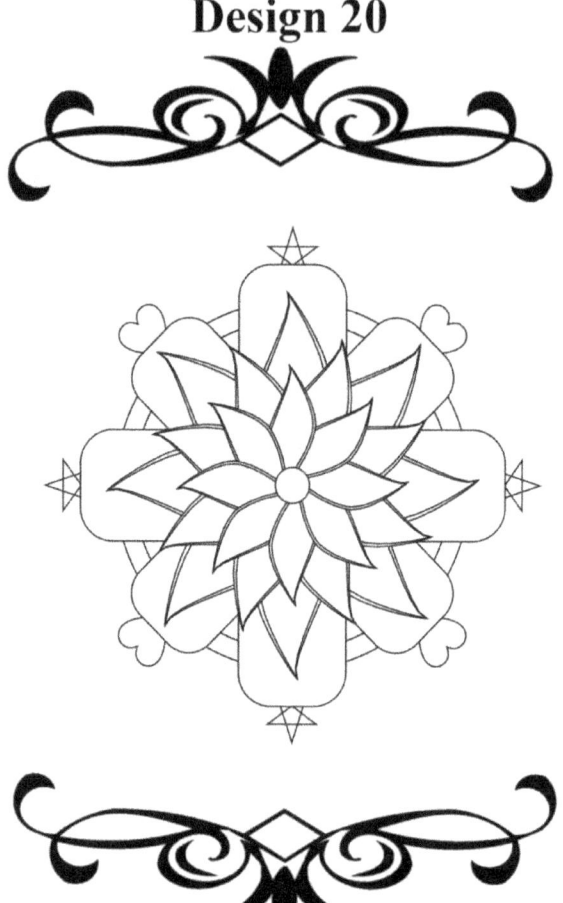

Design 21

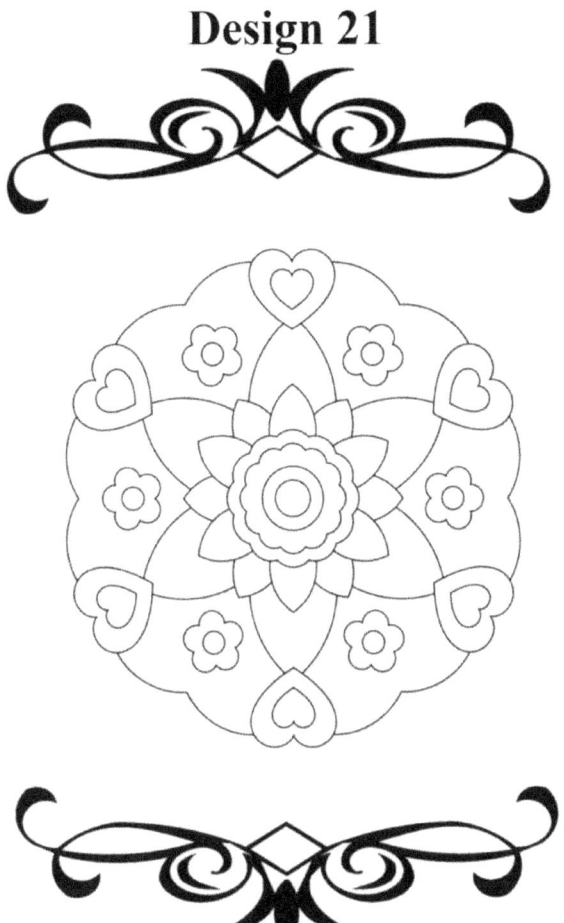

Design 22

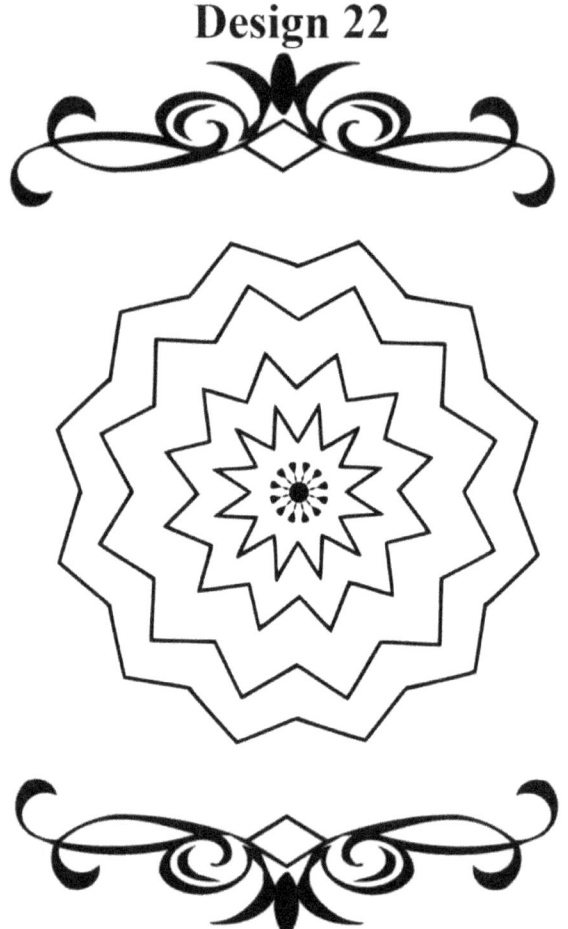

Design 23

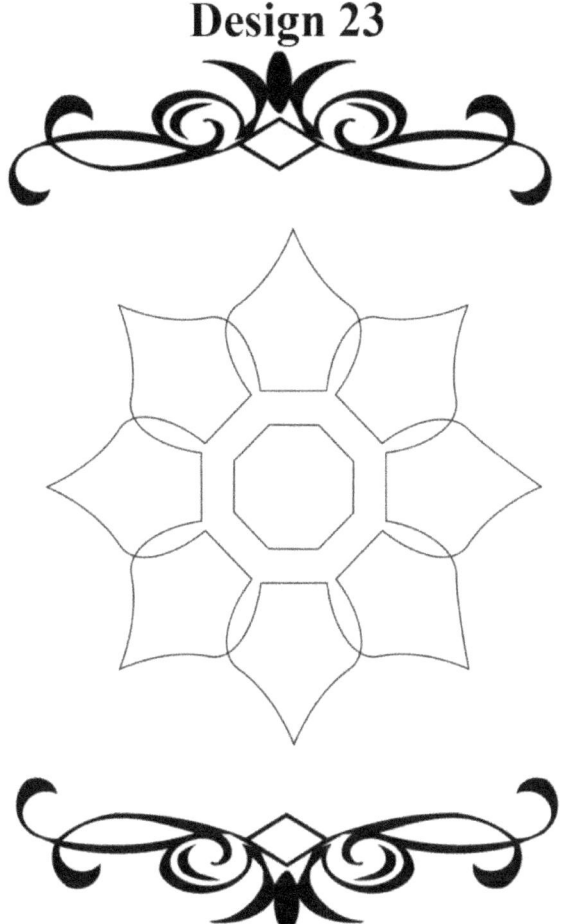

Design 24

Design 25

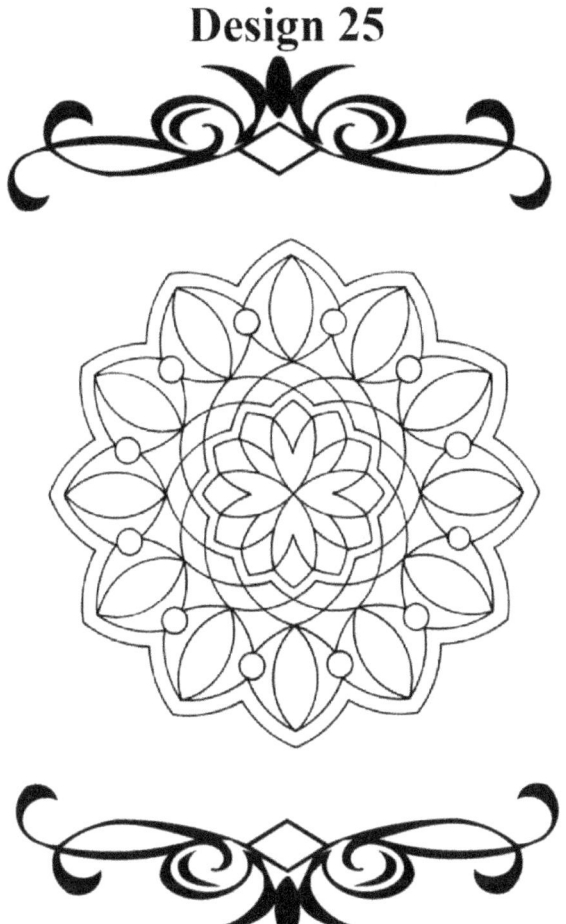

Design 26

Design 27

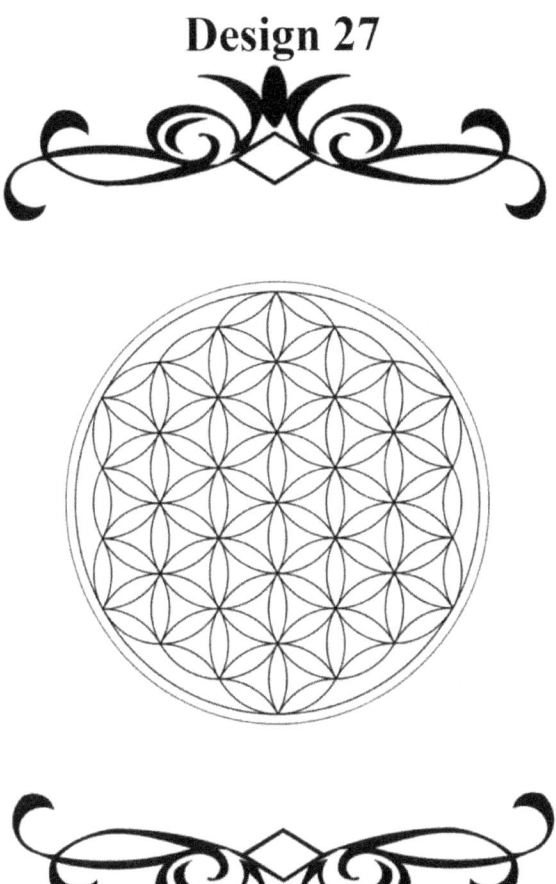

Design 28

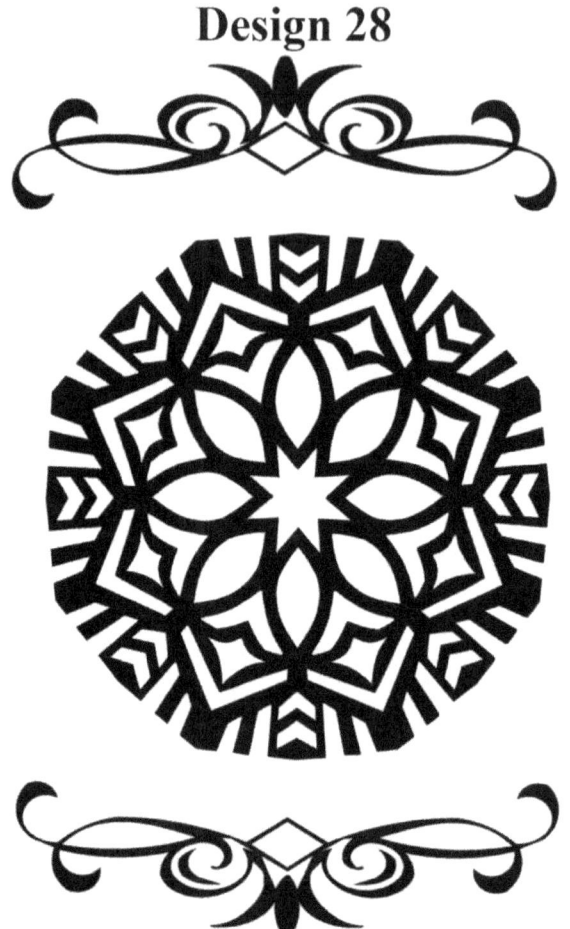

Design 29

Design 30

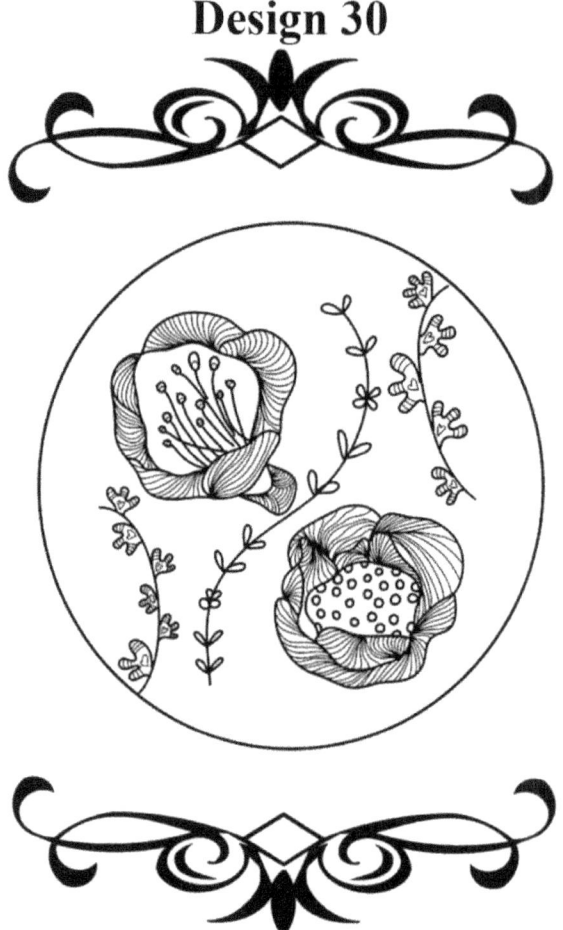